Romanticism

Théodore Géricault
Rouen 1791-Paris 1824
The Wounded Cuirassier, 1814
Oil on canvas 1′6″ × 1′3″
Paris, Musée du Louvre

Romanticism

PEEBLES ART LIBRARY   **Sandy Lesberg, Editor**

First published 1974
by
Peebles Press International
U.S.: 140 Riverside Drive, New York, N.Y. 10024
U.K.: 12 Thayer Street, London, W1M 5LD

ISBN 0-85690-032-X

The illustrations were provided by
André Held, Lausanne, except:
Giraudon, Paris: pages 8, 17, 22, 23, 28, 30, 31, 35, 39,
42, 44.
Hainelle, Paris: page 3.
Tate Gallery, London: page 26.

Distributed by
Walden Books, Resale Division in the
U.S. and Canada.
WHS Distributors in the U.K., Ireland,
Australia, New Zealand and South Africa.

Printed and Bound in Great Britain

Introduction

For the first twenty-five years of the 20th century, Romanticism was openly disparaged in France. And not merely Romanticism as an historical fact—Romanticism as a cultural phenomenon was also included. To understand this curiously scornful attitude one must necessarily consider several different facts: first, academic prejudice, so deeply rooted in France that, in spite of the passage of time, there is still a firm conviction that the finest and best French literature can be found only in the Classical writers of the age of Louis XIV and that Victor Hugo is basically only a babbling bore suitable for primary schools and free-thinkers. I suppose some might think that I am joking, but I genuinely believe that this idiotic prejudice, like so many others, is still firmly rooted in the orthodox subconscious. The second reason which I think may be responsible for the general disrepute of Romanticism in the years immediately preceding the first world war relates to the influence of reactionary opinion, especially that of the proto-Fascism of the Action Française. This led inevitably to revulsion against the so-called "stupid 19th century", a period born of the French Revolution and itself a succession of revolutions. Finally, one must acknowledge in a wider and more general sense the spirit of reaction itself, always present in man, and the tendency of men as a whole to dislike all historical changes which automatically bring with them a change of ideas, of behaviour and of emotional response. But, as Raymond Cogniat writes in this small but illuminating summary of Romanticism, a study remarkable for its power of synthesis and its crisp concision, in spite of this, what is done is done and "what society has acquired in this way is irrevocable". It is the irrevocableness which is hard to take. It must be accepted, though, as a basic fact of existence. Mere trends can be resisted—they are only passing fancies—but there is no way of resisting changes arising from an event as far-reaching, vast and decisive as the French Revolution; from it came a complete transformation of man's view of himself and of his powers. He was changed from subject into citizen, he saw himself fully participating in that creative force which is the people in action, he realised his own individuality and on this account saw that he was responsible for his own destiny as well as for the destiny of others. These were all completely new concepts, all as new as those arising from Christianity and the Renaissance. It was inevitable that they should produce changes in taste, emotion and creative spirit which were to be no less astonishing: they in turn produced Romanticism.

We should be grateful to Raymond Cogniat for starting his history of Romanticism with David. David was a Classical artist, taking the term in its proper sense and ignoring the implications of time and space. But this Classical artist was a contemporary of the French Revolution and was instantly revealed as a typical " new man", a modern man unrelated to any system of concepts of a fixed and unalterable nature, a man who participated fully in the drama of living—a drama which might sometimes be tricked out in antique garments while historical exploits, painted in former times in celebration of their prince and performer, appeared in contemporary costume, though beneath this they still looked like scenes from antiquity and indeed have all the appropriate grandeur and solemnity. Henceforward, historical painting has a completely new method of presentation: it is not an illustration of an event, it is the event itself, an actual happening. The Revolution produced a new concept of tragedy and this was to be found in the works of Gros, Goya, Géricault and Delacroix and in the novels of Stendhal and Balzac. It is a tragedy truly experienced: an heroic tragedy.

This heroism is not found only in the violence and the tumult of the century; in times of peace, it finds its place in the simple events of everyday life. This is the "heroism of modern life" analysed so clearly by Baudelaire and transformed by him into superb verse of melancholy stoicism. Romantic art does indeed last right up to this time and Baudelaire made no mistake when he listed so many of his works under this heading. Romantic art therefore includes the very special type of realism which was to be the typical realism of the mid-century and which Raymond Cogniat has included in his study.

Tragedy can be found everywhere. It is universal and omnipresent. It is living and lived, collective experience, personal experience, epic, lyric, the history of a nation through the eyes of Michelet, the history of a soul through the poetic and musical vision of Lamartine, Hugo, Musset, Berlioz, Liszt and Chopin. From all this sprang one of the vast revolutions whose field of operation is the human consciousness and which establish a new distribution of the faculties of the mind. One of these faculties became preponderant: exalted by Baudelaire and recognised by him as totally supreme in the art of Delacroix, it was the imagination. It reigned supreme in every part, a sovereign power, magical, wonderful. No one could start to conceive a history of modern times without first writing a monograph on the imagination, without analysing and defining in all its individuality this curious phenomenon of the human mind. Moreover, it is impossible to understand anything about the different stages in human evolution and the various cycles of civilisation if one does not examine the meaning each period gives to particular concepts which differ according to time and place: concepts such as imagination, reason and nature.

Romantic man, therefore—and modern man who came after him—has his own particular concepts. And through them, a specific potential of imaginative, creative, expressive and emotive power. There is always the danger that in certain cases this power will go above and beyond the realisation by which it should make itself concrete: indeed, sometimes it cancels it out entirely. Raymond Cogniat has shown that this danger exists in the work of Fuseli, an artist who, within his limits, has great charm and whose graphic works, like those of Blake, sometimes demonstrate a disastrous result, brought about by his exceptional inferiority and his formidable spiritual powers. In these cases of extreme Romanticism, imagination triumphs over realisation and goes beyond the form by which it should make itself manifest. In such cases, as Hegel says in his Aesthetics, *the content of Romantic art "by virtue of its free spirituality demands more than external and corporeal representation can give it". For every force risks its own destruction, the force of Romantic art just as much as that of Classical art, the force generated by any new adventure of the spirit.*

Romantic art is surely one of the most powerful and wonderful art forms to come from the mind of man. At each peak of achievement—and these were countless and splendid— it attained a true and marvellous humanism.

Jean Cassou

Jacques-Louis David
Portrait of Madame Récamier
Oil on canvas 5′8″ × 8′0″
Paris, Musée du Louvre

Francisco José de Goya y Lucientes
Fuendetodos 1746-Bordeaux 1828
The Burial of the Sardine
Oil on canvas 2′9″ × 2′0″
Madrid, Academia San Fernando

Gustave Courbet
Ornans 1819-La Tour-de-Peilz 1877
The Three Bathers
c. 1868
Oil on canvas 4′2″ × 3′2″
Paris, Musée du Petit-Palais

Dominique Ingres
The Turkish Bath, 1863
Oil on canvas 3'7″ diameter
Paris, Musée du Louvre

Jean-Auguste-Dominique Ingres
Montauban 1780-Paris 1867
Portrait of Mademoiselle Rivière
Oil on canvas 3'3″ × 2'4″
Paris, Musée du Louvre

Camille-Jean-Baptiste Corot
Paris 1796-Ville-d'Avray 1875
The Belfry at Douai
Oil on canvas 1'6" × 1'4"
Paris, Jeu de Paume

François-Pascal Gérard
Rome 1770-Paris 1837
Murat, King of Naples
Oil on canvas 7′0″ × 4′3″
Ravenna, Collection of the Count
Giovan Battista Spalletti Trivelli

Francisco Goya
Cardinal Don Luis Maria de Borbon y Vallabriga
c. 1798
Oil on canvas 6′6″ × 3′4″
São Paulo

Jacques-Louis David
Paris 1748-Brussels 1825
Marat assassinated
Oil on canvas 5′5″ × 4′2″
Brussels, Musée royal des Beaux-Arts

Théodore Géricault
The Madwoman
Oil on canvas 2′4″ × 1′11″
Lyons, Musée

Francisco Goya
The Churching, 1818-19
Oil on canvas 1′9″ × 2′6″
Agen, Musée municipal

Jacques-Louis David
Coronation of the Emperor Napoleon I
and Crowning of the Empress Josephine
in the Cathedral of Notre-Dame in Paris,
2 December 1804 (detail). Oil on canvas
Paris, Musée du Louvre

Francisco Goya
The Massacre of the Third of May
Oil on canvas 10′9″ × 11′2″
Madrid, Prado

Antoine-Jean Gros
Paris 1771-Bas-Meudon 1835
Bonaparte at Arcola, 17 November 1796
Oil on canvas 2′5″ × 1′11″
Paris, Musée du Louvre

Pierre-Paul Prud'hon
Cluny 1758-Paris 1823
Portrait of the Empress Josephine
Oil on canvas 8′0″ × 6′4″
Paris, Musée du Louvre

Eugène Delacroix
Dante and Virgil in Hell, 1822
Oil on canvas 6'3" × 7'8"
Paris, Musée du Louvre

Eugène Delacroix
The Massacres on Chios
Oil on canvas 13'10" × 11'7"
Paris, Musée du Louvre

Eugène Delacroix
Muley Abd er-Rahman,
Sultan of Morocco, 1845
Oil on canvas 12'4″ × 12'2″
Toulouse, Musée des Augustins

Eugène Delacroix
Liberty leading the People, 1830
Oil on canvas 8'7" × 10'8"
Paris, Musée du Louvre

John Constable
East Bergholt 1776-London 1837
Master James Heys
Oil on canvas 1′5″ × 1′1″
Winterthur, Reinhart Collection

Francisco Goya
La Maja vestida (1797-8)
Oil on canvas 3′1″ × 6′3″
Madrid, Prado

Francisco Goya
La Maja desnuda (1797-8)
Oil on canvas 3′2″ × 6′3″
Madrid, Prado

William Blake
London 1757-1827
God judging Adam
London, Tate Gallery

Camille Corot
The Woman with a Pearl, 1868-70
Oil on canvas 2′4″ × 1′9″
Paris, Jeu de Paume

Honoré Daumier
Marseilles 1808-79
Crispin and Scapin, *c.* 1860
Oil on canvas 2′0″ × 2′8″
Paris, Musée du Louvre

Nicolas-Toussaint Charlet
Paris 1792-1845
Two Old Soldiers after Waterloo
Oil on canvas 1′8″ × 1′4″
Private collection

Jean-François Millet
The Gleaners
Oil on canvas 1′9″ × 2′1″
Paris, Musée du Louvre

Jean-François Millet
The Angelus
Oil on canvas 1′9″ × 2′1″
Paris, Musée du Louvre

Gustave Courbet
Sleep, 1866
Paris, Musée du Petit-Palais

Gustave Courbet
The Outskirts of Ornans
Oil on canvas 1'4″ × 1'0″
Bulle, Musée Gruérien

Gustave Courbet
Young Ladies on the Banks of the Seine, 1856
Oil on canvas 5'8″ × 6'9″
Paris, Musée du Petit-Palais

Honoré Daumier
The Print Collector
c. 1857
Oil on canvas 1′4″ × 1′1″
Paris, Musée du Petit-Palais

Honoré Daumier
The Washerwoman
c. 1860
Oil on wood 1′7″ × 1′1″
Paris, Musée du Louvre

Honoré Daumier
The Burden
c. 1850
Oil on canvas 1′7″ × 1′3″
Prague, National Gallery

Louis-Léopold Boilly
La Bassée 1761-Paris 1845
The Grandfather's Birthday, 1818
Oil on canvas 1′0″ × 1′4″
Rome, Galeria d'arte antica
Palazzo Barberini

Eugène Delacroix
The Death of Sardanapalus, 1827
Oil on canvas 12′11″ × 14′2″
Paris, Musée du Louvre

Camille Corot
Normandy Landscape, 1822-4
Oil on canvas 6″ × 1′0″
Arlesheim, Stoll Collection

Camille Corot
The Reader on the Wooded Bank
Rheims, Musée des Beaux-Arts

Jean-Henri Fuseli
Zurich 1741-Putney 1825
The Small Fairy
Oil on canvas 2′1″ × 2′5″
Basle, Musée

Gustave Courbet
Courbet with a Black Dog, 1842
Oil on canvas 1′5″ × 1′9″
Paris, Musée du Petit-Palais

Charles Daubigny
Paris 1817-78
Seascape, 1866
Oil on wood 10" × 1′5″
Lyons, Musée

Théodore Rousseau
Paris 1812-Barbizon 1867
Storm Scene, View of the Montmartre Plain
Oil on canvas 8" × 1′2″
Paris, Musée du Louvre

Narcisse Diaz de la Peña
Bordeaux 1807-Menton 1876
Landscape
Oil on wood 1′0″ × 1′4″
Dijon, Musée

Antoine-Jean Gros
Battle at Nazareth
Oil on canvas 3'7" × 6'6"
Nantes, Musée des Beaux-Arts

Alexandre Calame
Vevey 1810-Menton 1864
View of Geneva
Oil on cardboard 1′0″ × 1′4″
Winterthur, Reinhart Collection

Dominique Ingres
La Baigneuse, 1808
Canvas 3′11 × 3′3″
Paris, Musée du Louvre

Théodore Géricault
The Epsom Derby, 1821
Oil on canvas 3'0" × 4'0"
Paris, Musée du Louvre

Théodore Géricault
Horse stopped by Slaves
c. 1817
Oil on canvas 1′6″ × 1′11″
Rouen, Musée des Beaux-Arts

Théodore Chassériau
Sleeping Nymph, 1850
Oil on canvas 4′5″ × 6′11″
Avignon, Musée Calvet

Glossary of Romanticism

Basire, James (1730-1802)

English engraver, born and died in London. He was one of the finest engravers of his time. He was the son of Isaac Basire, also an engraver; his son, James the younger, died in 1822 and was also an engraver and draughtsman of distinction. James the elder was a pupil of Richard Dalton. He travelled in Italy. On his return, he had a large number of commissions and became well known. He became a member of the Royal Society in 1770. He engraved a number of pictures including *The Life of Henry VIII* and *The Field of the Cloth of Gold.*

Bertin, Jean-Victor (1775-1842)

French painter, born and died in Paris. He was influenced by Poussin. His paintings were first exhibited at the 1793 Salon. He was famous under the Empire and the Restoration. He was one of Corot's teachers. Bertin brought back a considerable number of canvases and watercolours from his travels in Egypt and Greece: *Landscapes from the Banks of the Nile* (Rouen), *View from Mt Pieria in Macedonia over Dion* (Autun), etc. Most of his paintings are in French galleries and museums.

Blake, William (1757-1827)

English painter, poet and writer, born and died in London. He was the son of a draper. He was only ten years old when he started studying drawing in London. He learned engraving with Basire with whom he stayed for seven years. It was at this time that he was most influenced by Gothic architecture, starting with his studies of Westminster Abbey and other Gothic churches in London. Next he worked at the Royal Academy and studied Michelangelo. His first engravings come from this period: *Joseph of Arimathea in the Rocks of Albion* (1773) and *The Day of Happiness* (1780). After his marriage, he became even more involved with mysticism and fantasy. He wrote poems deeply imbued with a sense of the extraordinary and illustrated them himself: *Milton* and *Jerusalem.* He wrote many other poems—*To Spring, To the Evening Star,* etc. Together with Victor Hugo, Novalis and Fuseli, he is one of the great masters of the fantastic of his time. There are works by him in the National Gallery and the Manchester Art Gallery.

Bonington, Richard Parkes (1801-28)

Son of an English landscape painter who taught him to paint at an early age. Bonington first travelled in France when he was only fifteen. He studied the art of water-colour painting there and worked in the Louvre. He enrolled at the Beaux-Arts and had lessons from Gros. When he left the Beaux-Arts, he began travelling all over France, but mostly worked in Normandy, usually painting outdoors—*View from Lillebonne, View of Le Havre* (1824 Salon) and *View of Abbeville.* He went on to Flanders. He won a gold medal in France. His talent for lithography can be seen in the *Picturesque Travels in Old France* by Baron Taylor; he also painted the well-known *Rue de la Grosse-Horloge in Rouen.* On his return to England, he started painting historical pictures under the influence of Sir Walter Scott: *Francis I and the Queen of Navarre, Henri IV and the Spanish Ambassador*, etc. He travelled in Italy, visiting Rome, Florence, Milan and Venice: *View of the Grand Canal* and *The Palazzo Ducale in Venice*. But, eventually, he settled in Paris, in a studio in the Rue Saint-Lazare. He painted many pictures of the outskirts of Paris: *View of Meudon*, *Saint-Cloud*, etc. From time to time, he went back to England. He was a close friend of Delacroix. A short time after he died, Lawrence wrote: " I do not think that an untimely death has in our time robbed us of an artist whose talent promised more after such an astonishing and speedy development." Bonington was a painter of great talent; he may be considered the link between the French school and the English school, a simultaneous blend of Classicism and Romanticism. He was much influenced by Constable; his paintings are outstanding by virtue of their colour and an incomparable use of light which is peculiar to his work as a whole.

Boudin, Eugène-Louis (1824-98)

French painter born in Honfleur, died in Paris. He did not leave Le Havre till he was twenty-five, having started out in the paper trade; he went to Paris and studied painting under Isabey. He became a close friend of Baudelaire. From 1860 Boudin experimented with effects of light and luminous colours which led him to paint some almost abstract studies towards the end of his life. Together with Jongkind, who was working on the Norman coast at the same time, he can be counted as one of the forerunners of Impressionism. He did, in fact, join the Impressionists in 1875 and he knew Manet. He had some influence on the painters of his time and on such young artists as Friesz, Dufy and Braque. Most European galleries have at least one of his pictures.

Burne-Jones (Sir Edward Coley) (1833-98)

English painter, born in Birmingham, died in London. After a brilliant career at Oxford, he thought of entering the Church when he suddenly saw some drawings by Dante Gabriel Rossetti and decided to be an artist. He went to see Rossetti in London and showed him his first efforts. Rossetti gave him every encouragement. In 1859 he went to Italy and was deeply impressed by the Primitives. Back in London, he went on studying and it was not until 1877 that he had his first successes. He was essentially a religious, almost mystical, painter, adapting the mood and colours of Renaissance Italy to his English temperament. His works include: *The Mirror of Venus*, *The Annunciation*, seven paintings of *St George and the Dragon* and tapestry designs for William Morris. The main body of his work is to be found in England.

Carrière, Eugène (1849-1906)

French painter and engraver, born in Gournay near Paris, died in Paris. He was a pupil at the Paris Ecole des Beaux-Arts in 1870 and soon afterwards went to work in Cabanel's studio, where he learnt to express to the full the warm, gentle poetic side of his personality which appears in the best of his work. He painted the working classes and the sorrow lurking below the surface which is apparent in the lower strata of society at the end of the last century. His main works include: *The Young Mother*, *The Winders*, *The Sick Child*, and an outstanding *Christ crucified*, which is " one of the most dramatic interpretations ever produced in religious painting ". Carrière decorated the Hôtel de Ville in Paris and the Sorbonne. He was, in addition, a fine engraver. His works are scattered in various galleries all around the world: *Portrait of Verlaine* in Boston.

Cézanne, Paul (1839-1906)

French painter born in Aix-en-Provence, died there in 1906. One of the great masters of 19th-century painting, a precursor of Cubism. Paul Cézanne had a decisive influence on young painters at the start of the 20th century.

Chassériau, Théodore (1819-56)

French painter and engraver, born of French parents in South America, died in Paris. He was a pupil of Ingres at the Ecole des Beaux-Arts and studied there from 1833 onwards. He won the second gold medal at the 1844 Salon for his *Christ in the Garden*. Chassériau decorated a number of churches in Paris: Saint-Roch (Baptistery Chapel), Saint-Merri (St Mary the Egyptian chapel) and Saint-Philippe-du-Roulé (*Descent from the Cross*). His production was generally prolific: *Sabbath in the Jewish Quarter in Constantine*, *Desdemona*, *Moorish Women*, etc. Most of his paintings and drawings are in French museums: Paris (Louvre), Versailles, Le Havre, Avignon, Poitiers, Nantes and La Rochelle.

Chateaubriand (François-René de) (1768-1848)

French writer and diplomat, born at the Château de Combourg near Saint-Malo, died in Paris. It is difficult to discuss any aspect of Romanticism or Romantic art without mentioning Chateaubriand. He occupies a curious position astride the watershed between *ancien régime* and Restoration—but the Restoration was also the period of the Romantic revolt and for Chateaubriand, author of that Romantic tale *Atala*, it represented a moment full of hope as well as anxiety; he wrote in *Mémoires d'Outre-Tombe:* "I found myself between two centuries, as it were, at the junction of two great rivers; I plunged into their troubled waters. I looked with regret at the banks where I was born but I swam with hope to the new and unknown shore." His comments are, therefore, very valuable, especially when he pauses in the course of his memoirs to pass his opinions on a work of art or a piece of literature. Chateaubriand virtually lived two lives, but passed through five separate epochs: he saw the *ancien régime*, the Revolution, the Empire, the Restoration and, finally, the July Monarchy; one year more and he would have seen the Second Republic. His impressions of people and of things, therefore, have all the shrewdness of a man whose taste and sensitivity have been sharpened by experience and misfortune. Sometimes, he withholds his own comments and lets a third party speak: writing of Napoleon, he says: "Girodet had put the finishing touches to my portrait. He gave it a gloomy look, but he imbued it with sheer genius." M. Denon (Baron Denon, Director-General of Museums under the Empire) accepted the work for the 1808 Salon, but since Chateaubriand was out of favour he wisely set it on one side. When Napoleon came to see the paintings, he asked: "Where is Chateaubriand's portrait?" He knew that it had been accepted and Denon was obliged to bring it out for him to see. Bonaparte looked at it rather sourly and commented: "He looks like a conspirator who has just come down the chimney" (*Mémoires d'Outre-Tombe*, volume III, p. 7, Ed. Garnier). Some men do indeed have the gift of the perfect comment. Chateaubriand seems to have had a high opinion of Girodet (who illustrated his novel *Atala* with the famous burial picture now in the Louvre) since he wrote: "Unfortunately, I have not the skill of M. Girodet, and while he makes my pictures more beautiful, I am always afraid of spoiling his" (note to the first canto of *Les Martyrs*). He left us a whole series of anecdotes and comments on the works of David, Gérard and Girodet as well as other painters from the period of the Empire, mostly in the course of his *Mémoires*. He has little to say on the subject of Romanticism. He was in the diplomatic service by the end of the Hundred Days and stayed in politics till the end of his life. But Chateaubriand, who was deeply influenced by Rousseau and who by travelling in the land of the Natchez gave the finishing touch to the exoticism originally brought to Europe by Bernardin de Saint-Pierre, in his turn influenced the generation which prepared the way for Romanticism. Without Chateaubriand and English literature, which he introduced into France, many painters would have lacked the major part of their sources of inspiration. Apart from his own works, Chateaubriand and his close friends were the subjects for portraits which are considered among the finest works of some artists—the *Portrait of Madame Récamier* by Gérard, the *Portrait of Madame de Staël* by the same artist and the fantastic picture of Chateaubriand at the end of his life, which was painted by Antoine Etex, one of Ingres's pupils.

Constable, John (1776-1837)

English painter, born in East Bergholt, died in London. With Turner and Bonington, he was one of the greatest English landscape artists. He came from a well-established Suffolk family. He started life by studying for the Church and it was at the suggestion of Sir George Beaumont that his family sent him to London to study painting. He made rapid progress. His highly personal style and non-conformity did not attract the general public for some time and he was not elected an associate member of the Royal Academy till 1819. In 1824, some of his pictures crossed the Channel and caused a sensation in Paris. He had a great influence on French landscape painters, especially Théodore Rousseau and Jules Dupré. In 1828, he painted two of his masterpieces: *Salisbury Cathedral* and *The Farm in the Valley*, both in the National Gallery. He wrote his memoirs and a collection of letters. Most of the major art galleries in the world have examples of his paintings, but the finest are in London in the National Gallery and the Tate Gallery: *Weymouth Bay*, *Dedham Mill* (1820), *The Hay Wain*, *The Corn Field*, etc.

Corot, Camille-Jean-Baptiste (1796-1875)

French painter and engraver, born in Paris, died in Ville-d'Avray. One of the greatest French landscape painters. His father was a barber in the Rue du Bac. He and Madame Corot opened a dress shop which was extremely fashionable under the Directory. Camille was born during this period. Thanks to his father's contacts, he won a scholarship to the college at Rouen, but his desire to draw was so all-embracing that it was difficult for him to settle down to his formal studies. It was not long before he started painting. His father saw that it would be difficult to turn him away from his vocation and for this reason arranged for him to study in Bertin's studio. He painted in Rouen, Le Havre and Dieppe. It was at this time that his father bought a house at Ville-d'Avray and Corot went there to do some sketching. In 1826, he went to Rome where he worked for a year. He returned to France with a new flexibility of style and a new maturity. He went back to Italy in 1828 and stayed in Naples and Ischia. Then he went on a series of journeys through the different provinces of France: Ile-de-France, Burgundy, Picardy, Brittany, Auvergne and Normandy. In 1836, he stayed in Avignon. This period produced superb sketches which are frequently far better than many of his paintings. He had many admirers but did not lack harsh critics —as, for instance, the painter who said to one of his pupils: " Young man; you are making a mess of your work—you are painting as badly as Corot." Success did not come to him quickly, but after he won a gold medal at the 1848 Salon, his work became very fashionable. Napoleon III bought his *Souvenir of Marcoussis* (Louvre). Once he was famous, he was anxious to help younger painters: both Harpignies and Hervier owed their first steps in painting to him. Queen Victoria commissioned a painting from him. In 1871 he painted the *Belfry at Douai*, one of his masterpieces. He died a few years later at the height of his fame. His great skill and balanced temperament had a very profound influence on landscape painting in the second half of the 19th century.

Cotman, John Sell (1782-1842)

Painter of landscapes and seascapes, engraver, born in Norwich, died in London. In 1800, he settled in London. He exhibited at the Royal Academy as well as at the Water Colour Society. He travelled in Normandy where he did some splendid sketches of old Norman buildings in such ancient towns as Jumièges, Rouen, Dieppe and Bayeux. He was Professor of Drawing at King's College, London, from 1834 onwards. Cotman, equally great as a painter of seascapes, was, with John Crome, one of the finest representatives of the Norwich school. Almost all his works are in English galleries.

Courbet, Gustave (1819-77)

French painter, born in Ornans (Doubs),

died in La Tour-de-Peilz, Switzerland. After a bad start at the Collège Royal in Besançon, he went to Paris. He decided to concentrate entirely on painting and gained admittance to the studios of Hesse and Steuben. His first works were very deeply influenced by Romanticism; he painted pictures inspired by the works of Goethe (*Faust*, etc.), Victor Hugo and George Sand. Thanks to a *Self-portrait with a Dog*, he managed to have a painting accepted for the 1843 Salon; this was in fact one of his first outstanding works. Other paintings followed: *The Guitar Player* (1845), *The Man with the Belt* and *After Dinner at Ornans*. This last work was the one which made his reputation with the general public. Realism was born. This painting of four friends relaxing after a meal was a small revolution in painting. All the young writers were great admirers of his work, especially Baudelaire. A whole succession of paintings continued the trend: *The Peasants at Flagey* (1850), *The Stone Breakers* (1850) and the famous *Burial at Ornans*, also from the same year, now in the Louvre. This religious subject seemed to the public to be treated casually and created a scandal; they accused Courbet of " profaning a religious ceremony ". After a journey in the Midi in 1854 he painted yet another masterpiece: *The Meeting*. His colour range now grew much brighter and transparent; he seemed to abandon his heavier, coarser colours. He stayed on the Normandy coast on several occasions, at Etretat and Trouville. He met Whistler, Manet and Boudin. Some very fine landscapes date from this period: *The Cliff at Etretat* (1870) and *Stormy Sea* (1870) among them. He was an ardent supporter of the Commune in Paris and paid the penalty of exile for his support of those who overthrew the column in the Place Vendôme. He died in exile in Switzerland. His last works were not very good. Courbet had a very profound influence on late 19th-century painting, especially on painting in the Germanic countries. His works are scattered in museums and galleries all over the world.

Daubigny, Charles-François (1817-78)

French landscape painter, born and died in Paris. He belonged to a family of artists. He went to Rome at the age of seventeen. He spent a year there visiting all the galleries in Rome and the rest of Italy. At the age of twenty-one, he entered Delaroche's studio; he earned a living decorating chocolate boxes and drawing pictures for periodicals. He exhibited a *View of Notre-Dame de Paris* at the 1838 Salon and had some etchings in the 1840 and 1841 Salons. His landscapes now began to find some favour. In 1857 he decorated some rooms in the Louvre. He had a barge built for himself so that he could live on the water and paint in perfect freedom. He was enormously popular at this time. Daubigny produced a large number of paintings—too many, in fact, for he began to wear himself out and died of a heart complaint in 1878. Daubigny had an influence on such painters as Boudin, Jongkind, Courbet, Harpignies and Bastien Lepage. His pictures are found in all the main European galleries. The Tretiakov Gallery in Moscow has some of his finest landscapes: *The Banks of the Oise, The Sea Coast, Morning, A Little Village, Solitude* and *Evening at Honfleur.* A fine collection is in the Louvre.

Daumier, Honoré (1808-79)

Painter and lithographer, born in Marseilles. He had a number of jobs before he started taking drawing lessons, none of which seem to have taught him much. So he learnt lithography and continued with his drawings. He achieved a remarkable brio in his drawing technique; in 1830 he worked on the periodical *La Silhouette.* At the end of the same year, he started drawing for *La Caricature,* an opposition paper. One of his first satirical drawings, *Gargantua,* got him six months in prison. When he came out, he carried on with his caricatures, followed parliamentary sessions, took sketches and, when he was back home in the evenings, produced portraits of deputies and ministers in the form of clay figures, astonishingly lifelike. In 1834 he produced the magnificent lithograph *The Massacre of Rue Transnonain;* soon afterwards he engraved *The Burial of La Fayette.* He worked for the *Charivari,* for which he drew his splendid series on *The Good Bourgeois, The Artists, The Legal Profession,* etc. He also produced some remarkable drawings such as *Don Quixote* and characters from the *commedia dell' arte.* His *Don Quixote and Sancho Panza* is in Berlin. Daumier was a passionate defender of liberty, an adversary of the régimes of Louis-Philippe and Napoleon III; he foresaw the war of 1870 and engraved a series of plates which give a foretaste of what was to appear in *Actualités.* Balzac, Baudelaire and Banville praised his enormous skill. Michelet was his friend. He became blind at the end of his life and died in poverty, living on the meagre pension allotted to him by the State and the gifts of his friends—Corot was particularly generous and gave him a house in the country. Georges Duhamel was to write of him: "The people he painted are 19th-century people by their clothes; but by their characteristics and attitudes, they are people of all time. I cannot help thinking that if I could draw, this is exactly how I should draw my contemporaries." Among Daumier's works, now scattered all over the world, one should mention: Amsterdam, *Christ and His Disciples, Two People singing;* Berlin, *Don Quixote and Sancho Panza;*

The Hague (Mesdag Museum), *The Gossip*; New York (Metropolitan Museum), *A Third-class Carriage*, *The Amateur*, *Palaisse*; Paris (Louvre), *The Robbers and the Donkey*, *Portrait of the Artist Théodore Rousseau*, *The Republic* (1848), *The Laundrywoman*, *Crispin and Scapin*, *Scenes from the Play*, *The Gipsy Procession*, etc.; Paris (Petit Palais), *The Print Collector*, *The Emigrants*; Montreal, *Peasant Feast*; and Munich, *The Melodrama*.

David, Jacques-Louis (1748-1825)

French painter, born in Paris, died in Brussels. His family were very anxious for him to enter Boucher's studio, but the old painter did not wish to take any new pupils; he suggested that David should go to Vien. He missed the Prix de Rome twice, but won it in 1774. When the Revolution came, David followed the extremist line and voted for the death of Louis XVI. Under the Directory, he became a member of the Institut. Napoleon appointed him first court painter shortly after his coronation. David painted many portraits, historical and mythological pictures. David was immensely talented and had much influence on artists in the first half of the 19th century. He reacted strongly against 18th-century Mannerism and his natural dogmatism turned him towards the revolutionary Romantic movement. But David was a man of high passions and subject to all sorts of internal contradictions, as André Maurois discovered. Maurois wrote: "David was an outstanding example of an artist who could have produced one masterpiece after another if he had only listened to the dictates of his own talent, but who instead spent much of his life chasing ideas which were not really made to fit this talent. David the portrait-painter, the impeccable realist, the artist of unfailing good taste, seemed made to form

the natural link between 18th- and 19th-century art, to be the natural ancestor of Ingres, Manet and Degas, and it is in fact on this account that David is so important. But *he* believed that his true calling was the re-creation of the world of Greece and Rome. . . ." Most of David's works are to be found in Paris and provincial museums in France.

Decamps, Alexandre-Gabriel (1803-60)

French painter and lithographer, born in Paris, died in Fontainebleau. This artist is little known at the present time—which is a pity, because he has sufficient depth of talent to be considered a painter of real value. He came from a Picard family (he spent most of his childhood in a rustic semi-solitude) and entered Bouchot's studio when he went to Paris; his youthful talent made him instantly noticeable. He left Bouchot to go to Abel de Pujol, who undid the work of his previous teacher. After many journeys in Italy, the Middle East and the Balkans, he settled in Paris where he exhibited for the first time at the 1827 Salon. The general public did not care for his paintings, but he received the unstinted admiration of the non-establishment critics. From many points of view, Decamps stood on the threshold of the world of the Impressionists and of Cézanne. He exhibited again at the Paris Salons of 1831, 1843, 1845 and 1851. His works are scattered all over the world and can be seen in the Rijksmuseum in Amsterdam, the Mesdag Museum in The Hague, the Frankfurt Museum, the Tretiakov Collection in Moscow, the Wallace Collection in London, the Glasgow Art Gallery and the Louvre and the Musée des Arts Décoratifs in Paris.

Delacroix, Eugène (1798-1863)

French painter, engraver and lithographer, born in Charenton, died in Paris. His father was a minister under the Empire, and a prefect of Marseilles and Bordeaux, but left little money when he died. The artist had a difficult childhood; moreover, his talent developed late and it was not until 1816—apparently after he had seen a painting by Goya which he greatly admired—that he started painting. He entered Guérin's studio but his master made it abundantly clear that he thought his talent very mediocre. Delacroix, however, soon revealed his artistic capabilities and rapidly became famous both as painter and caricaturist. "Then Delacroix appeared," wrote René Huyghe, "and in one magnificent swoop gave pictorial Romanticism the language it sought, a language able to express its basic needs and its intensity. What Gros and Géricault had started, Delacroix carried through; instead of hard, precise contours which sought to fix form permanent and still in its perfection, he went on to use a line imbued with vigour and dynamic suggestion; his use of colour was not to satisfy ideas but to stir the emotions, the artist's chosen instrument. In this paradoxical way, this Romanticism, by means of which the Germany of *Sturm und Drang* sought to eliminate the hegemony of France, found through the genius of a French artist the expression it lacked. Delacroix brought it to bear on the passionate dreams and longings of Anglo-Saxon and Germanic men of genius, of Shakespeare, Byron, Schiller and Goethe." In 1830 he was acknowledged as the leader of the new school of painting. In spite of—or because of—his powerful originality, he was constantly attacked by more conventional painters, by Ingres in particular, and by the administration of the Beaux-Arts. In 1832, he went with the Comte de Mornay, the French ambassador, to travel through Morocco and Algeria. The journey had a great influence on him. At the instigation of Thiers, he decorated the "Salon du Roi" in the Palais Bourbon (1833) and the libraries of Luxembourg and the old Hôtel de Ville. He painted a fresco for a chapel in Saint-Sulpice: *Jacob struggling with the Angel*. His genius was officially recognised at the Universal Exhibition of 1855, where a whole room was given up to 35 of his most typical paintings. He was received as a member of the Institut in 1857. Too much hard work exhausted Delacroix prematurely and it was at this time that he was obliged to abandon some of his larger projects. Delacroix's paintings baffled many of his "established" contemporaries, but found a ready response among such younger painters as Manet, Whistler, Fantin-Latour and Monet.

Delaroche, Paul (1797-1856)

History painter, born and died in Paris. He was a pupil of Gros and a friend of Géricault. He became known when two of his pictures were shown at the 1822 Salon: *The Descent from the Cross* and *Joas saved by Josabeth*, but it was not till after 1830 that he grew really famous. In 1832 he was made a member of the Institut where he occupied the seat which Delacroix was to take after his death. In 1834, the Government commissioned him to decorate the Madeleine, but instead, Delaroche got married and went to Italy: the work was given to Ziegler instead. Some of the work was deliberately left for Delaroche to finish, but he was not unduly interested in it. A few years later, he gave up all official commissions to devote himself exclusively to his chosen field of historical painting. He had started as early as 1824 and produced such pictures as *Joan of Arc questioned in her Prison Cell by the Cardinal of Winchester* (Wallace Collection, London), *The Death of the Duc de Guise* (Wallace Collection), *Moses rescued from the Nile* (Amsterdam, Rijksmuseum), *Herod's Daughter* (Municipal

Museum, Cologne), *Mater Dolorosa* (Liège Museum), *Napoleon crossing the St Bernard* (Liverpool Art Gallery), *The Death of Queen Elizabeth* and *The Children of Edward* (Paris, Louvre). His output was enormous. In 1837, he started painting the hemicycle of the Palais-Bourbon, but died before it could be completed. Delaroche was an artist with a wide range and the few pieces of sculpture and modelling he did show that he did not lack talent in this field either.

Doré, Gustave (1832-83)

Painter, sculptor, engraver, black-and-white artist; born in Strasbourg, died in Paris. One of the truly great talents in drawing, but only a mediocre painter. He worked for the *Journal pour Rire*. In 1854 he started the illustrations of great works of literature which were to make him famous: *Gargantua*, La Fontaine's *Fables*, Balzac's *Contes drolatiques*, *The Divine Comedy* and *Orlando Furioso*. His pictures include: *Tobias and the Angel*, *The Neophyte* and *Francesca da Rimini*. Gustave Doré also sculpted part of the statue of Alexandre Dumas in the Place Malesherbes in Paris. Many of his pictures are in French museums.

Dupré, Jules (1811-89)

French painter and engraver, born in Nantes, died on the Isle-Adam, near Paris. His father had started life as a painter but went on to found a china factory at Creil. To please his father, the young Dupré tried to settle to painting plate decorations and then went on to work in another factory his father had started in Saint-Yriex in the Limousin. Here, Dupré gave up more and more of his time to painting for himself. He exhibited for the first time at the 1831 Salon. He travelled in England where he met Turner, Constable, Crome and Bonington; he was deeply influenced by them. Jules Dupré's career was successful and extremely hard-working; moreover, he was very much an innovator and brought a new dimension to the study of planes and colour; this contributed very largely to the new techniques which allowed Impressionist artists to develop their vision of nature and everyday things. He was also successful in the way he expressed fantasy and dreams and managed, by his use of space, to transcend even these elements. Even though he was uneven as a painter and though his skill could not always keep step with his ideas, he was, nevertheless, a superb technician with great subtlety of intuition. His works are in Amsterdam, The Hague, Stockholm, Breslau and Paris (Louvre).

Fromentin, Eugène (1820-76)

French painter and writer, born in La Rochelle. Son of a doctor who was fond of painting, he was a brilliant student at the Lycée in La Rochelle and came to Paris to read successfully for a degree in law. At the same time, he wrote poems and articles on modern literature and painting in the Paris newspapers and periodicals. He started painting with the approval of his family. In 1842 he entered the studios of Rémond and Cabat. He went to Algeria a short time afterwards and continued to perfect his style. He was to visit Africa twice more. His last visit, with his wife, lasted for two years. He brought back several pictures and some literary works: *A Summer in the Sahara* and *A Year in the Sahel*. His famous novel *Dominique* appeared two years later. He wrote a very fine work of art criticism: *Les Maîtres d'Autrefois*. Fromentin, whose talent as a landscape artist was quickly acknowledged, exhibited at the 1867 and 1873 Salons. Without being a truly great painter, far below the genius of Corot, too facile in technique to be an artist of depth, Fromentin was, even so, very gifted. Apart from two works—*The Banks of the Nile* in Moscow and *In the Land of Thirst* in Brussels—all his paintings are in private collections or in French provincial museums.

Fuseli, Jean (1741-1825)

Swiss portrait painter and art critic, born in Zurich, died in Putney, England. He started studying theology against his personal wishes but for the sake of pleasing his father. He gave it up after two years. Fuseli became a very close friend of Lavater. He began travelling about Europe, painting as he went, and visiting Berlin, Paris, London and Italy. He returned to England in 1779 and exhibited at the Royal Academy: *Nightmare*. He was recommended to the royal family by Sir Joshua Reynolds. He became very famous indeed and commissions poured in. He was appointed a professor of painting at the Royal Academy in 1799, having been an academician since 1790. Fuseli was particularly gifted in rendering emotions—the tenderest as well as the most fantastical. He illustrated part of the works of Shakespeare and Milton. He also painted a number of pictures on Biblical themes. His works are in private collections and in the principal English museums and galleries.

Gavarni (Guillaume Chevalier, known as Paul) (1804-66)

French black-and-white artist and lithographer, born and died in Paris. He started illustrating books for a living rather late—it was a water-colour which he sent to the 1829 Salon which made his name. His drawings are elegant and have a genuinely Parisian touch: they soon established his reputation. He worked for all the famous periodicals of the time: *Le Charivari*, *La Mode*, *Silhouette*, etc. He exhibited at the Royal Academy in 1850. His works include the charmingly satirical drawings: *The Deceits of Women in Matters of the Heart*.

Gérard, François (Baron) (1770-1837)

History painter and portrait painter. Born into a modest family (his father was steward to Admiral Suffren), Gérard was admitted to the royal school of painting as a mark of royal patronage. It did not take him long to develop his talent and in 1786 he entered David's studio. Thanks to David, he managed to avoid national service under the Revolution and became a judge on the Committee of Public Safety instead of becoming a soldier. He returned to painting after Thermidor. Under the Directory, he made his name with *Belisarius*, exhibited at the 1795 Salon, then with *Love and Psyche* (1798 Salon). Napoleon took him into his service: he commissioned various paintings, one of which was *The Battle of Austerlitz*. A few years later, Gérard was made a Baron. He was introduced to Louis XVIII by Talleyrand after Waterloo and became the official painter of the Restoration—Louis XVIII overlooked the revolutionary to concentrate on the artist. Gérard painted portraits of the Bourbon and Orléans families and did various historical compositions such as *Henri IV entering Paris* and *The Coronation of Charles X*. Most of his works are in the Versailles Museum; some paintings are in the Louvre, others in provincial museums.

Géricault, Théodore (1791-1824)

French painter, sculptor and lithographer, born in Rouen, died in Paris. He came from a well-established Rouen family and gave up his formal education to enter

Carle Vernet's studio, leaving it to work with Guérin. He became an animal painter and began his famous series of pictures of horses, at the same time devoting much of his time to portraits and history paintings. After serving for a time with the musketeers in one of Louis XVIII's regiments, he went to Italy where he visited Rome and Florence. On his return he painted his famous *Raft of the Medusa* (Louvre). " At the beginning," wrote Pierre Courthion, " there is a sort of soldierly vehemence about Géricault, the same epic exaltation as you find in Gros. In a way, he is the Rouennais counterpart of Heinrich Heine, the young Rhenish poet whose head was turned by the Grande Armée. But after the shock of Waterloo, the image of the fallen cuirassier haunted his fancy and he saw in the uniform of the red musketeers, Louis XVIII's regiment in which he took service, a means of finding and keeping an attitude. But this was not enough to cure him of the great thwarted love which still troubled him. 'I look in vain for something to lean on,' he wrote to his former fellow-student Dedreux-Dorcy, a friend of long-standing, 'but nothing is solid, everything slips away from me, everything deceives me. All our hopes and longings on this earth are only vain fancies and our successes are imaginary: we only think we have them. If there is anything on earth that is certain, then it is what we suffer. Suffering is real, pleasure is sheer fantasy.'" Géricault was a friend of Delacroix and the leader of the younger Romantics. This great artist died too young; he left portraits which were admirable in their astonishing and sometimes terrible reality: *Portrait of an Old Woman* (Le Havre), *Naked Women* (Rouen) and *Head of an Executed Man* (Geneva). Most of his works are in French museums, apart from *Cavalry Skirmish* in the Wallace Collection (London), *Horse Studies* (The Hague) and some in Geneva.

Goya y Luceintes (Francisco José de) (1746-1828)

Spanish painter, born in the province of Aragón, died in Bordeaux. After a tumultuous start to life (he was seriously wounded by a knife thrust after a brawl when coming out of a tavern), he went to Italy and started painting to please his fancy. He was driven out of the Papal States for having tried to carry off a nun. On his return to Madrid, he painted his first masterpieces: *The Carnival*, *The Flagellation*, *A Sitting of the Inquisition Tribunal*, *The Inside of a Madhouse*, etc., and produced some superb etchings. Goya, one of the very greatest Spanish painters, was an ardent Liberal and was very popular among the poor classes. Towards the end of his life, the artist asked permission from Ferdinand VI, whose official painter he was, to leave the country and he settled in Bordeaux. He was to die there not long afterwards.

He was an artist of extremely complicated temperament, shifting constantly and imperceptibly from gentle to positively satanic. The first part of his work is 18th-century-orientated, but the second is definitely Romantic in inclination: the definitions seem arbitrary, however. Vassily Photiades has studied the problem closely and comments: " Goya is Janus in person. The 'double man' finds in him the perfect expression of our duality. We do not necessarily refer only to the two periods of his life, to the Goya who reflects the charms of the 18th century (even though his strong personality shines through all the time) who is followed by the Goya who suddenly springs forth after a serious illness and towards his forty-third year. For the second period itself is full of contrasts: simultaneously gentle and cruel, his work seems to follow willingly one trend after another." This alternation of sentiment is at the root of Goya's particular genius, offering cruelty and tenderness, brutality and charm. "The unexpected charm of a pink and black jewel", Baudelaire was to write of Lola de Valencia. There are paintings by Goya in all the principal museums in the world: some forty are in the Prado (Madrid); the Louvre has *Woman with a Fan* and *Young Spanish Girl*; there are others in the National Gallery in London, at the Metropolian Museum, New York, Berlin (Kaiser-Friedrich-Museum) as well as in some provincial museums in France: *The Garrotte* (Lille), *The Grotesque Marriage* (Besançon), etc.

Gros, Antoine-Jean (Baron) (1771-1835)

French painter, born in Paris. At the age of fifteen, he entered David's studio. After an unlucky attempt at the Prix de Rome and a change in fortune which forced him to give lessons in order to survive as a painter, he went to Italy. Here, he had the good luck to meet Bonaparte. He began to specialise in history paintings and painted *The Battle of Arcola* which Bonaparte had engraved by Longhi. He was then invited to choose paintings to be taken to Paris for the Louvre. Gros became one of the best-known artists of the Empire period. His best works include: *The Plague-stricken at Jaffa*, *The Battle of Eylau* and *Napoleon meeting the Emperor of Austria after the Battle of Austerlitz*. He supported the Restoration but nevertheless was a great defender of David and did his best to persuade him to return to France from his exile in Brussels. Gros fell ill and suffered very greatly from the harsh criticism of his adversaries; he committed suicide by drowning himself in a pool near Meudon. His works are in the Louvre in Paris, in particular historical paintings and portraits of people of note during the Empire: *Eugène de Beauharnais*, *Jérôme Bonaparte*, *Duroc*, *Daru*, etc.

Guérin, Pierre-Narcisse (Baron) (1774-1833)

French painter, born in Paris and died in Rome. One of the rare instances of an artist who never showed any real inclination for art and who considered painting as nothing more than a job of work. His family practically had to force him to paint. He was sent to Brenet's studio, but it was Regnault who took him over and discovered his talent, forcing him to work in spite of his inherent laziness. Then all of a sudden he began liking what he was doing and won a prize (1797). His real career started first with the Directory and then with the Empire. The works he produced then were very typical of his natural style: theatrical and rather cold, but technically superb (*Phèdre accusing Hippolyte before Theseus*, *Andromache*, *Dido*, *Clytemnestra*, etc.). He was ennobled by the Emperor as were Gros and Gérard. His paintings are in French museums—a sketch in Madrid.

Ingres, Dominique (1780-1867)

French painter and engraver, born in Montauban and died in Paris. He showed his talent for drawing at a very early age and his father sent him to the Ecole des Beaux-Arts in Toulouse. When he was sixteen he went to study with David. Won the Prix de Rome in 1801 with his painting of *Achilles receiving Agamemnon's Messengers in his Tent*. In 1806 he exhibited a *Portrait of Napoleon on his Throne*. He went to Rome and painted various important works: *La Baigneuse* (1806), *Œdipus and the Sphinx* (1808), *Jupiter and Thetis*, *Virgil reading the Aeneid to Augustus*, *The Sleep of Ossian*, etc. He did not return to Paris until 1824; the pictures he exhibited caused a sensation: *The Vow of Louis XIII* (Montauban Cathedral), *Francis I with the Dying Leonardo da Vinci* and some portraits. The Classical painters who needed a figurehead to lead them in opposition to such young Romantics as Delacroix and Géricault—David being out of France—found him in the person of Ingres. Ingres, whose haughty, disdainful nature awoke very strong animosities—even violent hatred—had a profound influence on such young artists as Chassériau and Hippolyte Flandrin. But he was truest to himself in his drawings. Claude-Roger Marx wrote: " The purity of his pencil line tears us away from all Romanticism. There is very little here that is relative—only certain details of hair styles, furniture or clothing, and the instant obedience of women subjects to the dictates of fashion. No one could be more absolute, more firmly in the eternal, than Ingres, simultaneously a contemporary of Raphael, Holbein and Clouet, as his disciple Degas was to be and, even later, Toulouse-Lautrec. His line is firm yet vibrant and seems barely to touch the white paper. No colour creeps in to distract the eye." Ingres was elected a member of the Institut in 1825 and later became a member of the Academies of Berlin, Amsterdam, Munich and Florence. Commander of the Legion of Honour in 1845; Grand Officer of the Order of Prussia and of the Order of Leopold of Belgium. At the Exposition Universelle in 1855, his paintings—among them *The Apotheosis of Homer* (Louvre) —were immensely successful. His works are in the principal museums of Europe.

Jongkind, Jean Barthold (1819-91)

Dutch painter, born in Latrop near Rotterdam, died in La Côte-Saint-André (Isère). It was at the inauguration of the statue of William the Conqueror at Falaise (1845) that he met Isabey. From then onwards, Jongkind divided his time between Holland and France. His life was often troubled by financial difficulties and

at such times he was helped by Corot, Isabey, Rousseau and Bonvin. In 1863, he exhibited with Whistler and Fantin-Latour. He painted superb views of Holland and of the French coast, especially the Norman coastline. He stayed for a time at Honfleur where he met Monet, Boudin and Baudelaire. He found a close companion in the person of Madame Fesser who saved him from his passion for strong drink and helped calm his persecution mania. The critic Claude-Roger Marx wrote: " It would not be going too far if Jongkind were related to Van Goyen, Ruysdael and—more especially—to Rembrandt; the graphic brilliance of his etchings is very reminiscent of the latter." In his oil paintings, Jongkind is uneven in performance, but his water-colours are always very fine. His main works are in the Louvre (the Moreau-Nelaton and the Camondo Bequests), in Amsterdam, Rotterdam and Brussels.

Lawrence (Sir Thomas) (1769-1830)

English portrait painter. Son of an innkeeper, he showed talent for drawing at an early age—it is said that he spent his time in his father's inn making sketches of the customers. His father sent him to the Royal Academy school where he was very successful. His works were soon on exhibition. Sir Joshua Reynolds took an interest in him and advised him on his future. He took a short trip to France. In 1815, the Prince Regent commissioned him to paint people who had distinguished themselves in the Napoleonic wars. In about 1825, he visited France again and painted portraits of Charles X, the Dauphin and the Duc de Richelieu. He was an ardent collector and had a fine collection of drawings which were worth a small fortune even during his lifetime. Sir Thomas Lawrence was one of the very finest English portrait painters. His best works include: *John Julius Anger-*

stein (National Gallery, London), *George IV* (Wallace Collection, London), *Lord Whitworth* (Louvre), *Willem Ferdinand* (Rijksmuseum, Amsterdam), *Lord Pitt* (Hanover Museum), *Duc de Richelieu* (Besançon Museum), *Countess of Darnley* (Liverpool), etc.

Manet, Edouard (1832-83)

French painter, born and died in Paris, one of the outstanding members of the French school in the 19th century. He had a very profound influence on the painters of his time, especially after 1870. He was a friend of Baudelaire, Zola and Mallarmé. His works are in all the major museums of the world.

Millet, Jean-François (1814-75)

French painter, born in Gruchy, near Cherbourg, died in Barbizon. He was born into a family of peasants who had a small farm in the canton of Gréville. He soon showed outstanding skill in drawing. The town of Cherbourg gave him a yearly allowance to go to Paris to study art. He went into Delaroche's studio; he was twenty-three years old and he almost won the Prix de Rome that same year. After his wife died, he found life in Paris very difficult and he was very unhappy. He went back to the countryside where he had grown up and worked in Cherbourg and the surrounding districts; he painted shop-signs. He had little success before about 1860. The art dealer Stevens took all his paintings in return for a monthly allowance of a thousand francs in gold for three years. This meant the end of Millet's financial problems and made it possible for him to settle with his family in Barbizon (he had remarried by this time). From this period come *The Sower*, *Stooking* (Louvre), *The Gleaners*, *The Angelus* and *Night*, to mention only the most outstanding. He was about to take part in the decoration of the Pantheon when he died in 1875. Millet's work was more or less ignored in the early 20th century; his output was prodigious and his paintings are to be found in all the main museums of the world.

Monet, Claude (1840-1926)

French painter, from Le Havre like Friesz and Dufy. Very much influenced by his early training with Boudin, he went to Paris and worked with Renoir, Sisley and Frédéric Bazille. They were the first Impressionists. Claude Monet holds an important position among painters at the end of the last century and also, though in quite a different way, during the first twenty-five years of this century.

Moreau, Gustave (1826-89)

French painter, born and died in Paris. Student at the Ecole des Beaux-Arts, then studied with Picot in 1846. He exhibited his first work, a *Pietà*, at the 1852 Salon. His work was brilliantly bold in both colour and concept and was violently attacked by official criticism. He went on exhibiting, however: *Jason* in 1865; *The Young Man and Death* in 1866; and *Prometheus, Jupiter and Europa* in 1876. He was elected a member of the Institut in 1889. Gustave Moreau was a very typical painter from the second half of the 19th century. A visionary given to meditation, now mystical, now sensual, classical in technique and a good twenty years ahead of his time in his ideas, Moreau was a forerunner of surrealism and abstract art. He has had a considerable influence on modern painting. His studio produced the young painters who were later to be known as the Fauves: Matisse, Rouault, Marquet, Manguin, Camoin, Desvallières, Flandrin, Bussy, Piot, Milcendeau and Sérusier. Gustave Moreau bequeathed his home and all the paintings, sketches and water-colours in it to the State—over 18,000 drawings as well, many of outstanding artistic merit. His works are found in museums all over the world.

Prud'hon, Pierre-Paul (1758-1823)

French painter; he was born in Cluny and in 1780 went to Paris. He enrolled at the Académie school in the Rue Verneuil. He won the Etats de Bourgogne prize and this allowed him to go to Rome where he was deeply impressed by the work of Raphael and Leonardo da Vinci. These artists were his favourite painters all his life; his own work shows their influence very clearly. During the Revolution, he found life hard and the little work he was able to do brought in barely enough for him to support his wife. Once the worst was over, he started painting again and his very real artistic merits were appreciated. He became the drawing teacher of the Empress Marie Louise. Meanwhile, his wife had been impossible to live with and he had left her. He found happiness with Constance Mayer, one of his best pupils. It was a happiness that ended all too soon with Constance's suicide. Prud'hon died of grief a short time afterwards.

Raffet, Auguste (1804-60)

French painter and engraver, black-and-white artist. A difficult childhood was followed by his apprenticeship to a wood-turner, studying painting in the evenings. His gift for drawing won him entry to Charlet's studio and then to Gros's. His failure to win the Prix de Rome in 1831 turned him against painting and he decided to specialise in drawing and engraving. He began his fine series of battle scenes from the days of the Revolution and the Empire: *Representative of the*

People with the Army of the Rhine, *The Night Review*, *Long Live the Emperor* and *The Last Charge of the Red Banners*.

Redon, Odilon (1840-1916)

French painter, pastellist and lithographer, born in Bordeaux, died in Paris. Although Odilon Redon was of the same generation as the Impressionists—born in the same year as Monet, a year younger than Renoir and Sisley—he was never involved with them. As early as 1868 he wrote an article on the Salon saying: "Some artists want to restrict painting to the reproduction of what they see and nothing more. Those who restrict themselves to these limits condemn themselves to an inferior ideal. The great masters prove that once the artist is in full possession of his own personal style and his own way of painting, he is free to take his subjects from history, poetry, his own imagination. . . . " And Redon's imagination provided him with all he needed: the fantasy and fairy-tale inspiration of the dream. His world, rich in this dream-like beauty, defies definition, but it never lacks the careful structure imposed by his power of observation, especially his observation of nature. Redon was a disciple of Gérôme—but an even more ardent follower of the great botanist Clavand. His strange visions, his other-worldly characters, sometimes nightmarish in appearance, live and move in a world of flowers which recalls, curiously enough, the art of China. André Fontainas described them: "The delicate pastels of a visionary, pictures where a vivid, multi-coloured background reveals the brilliant corolla of dream-flowers and real flowers; over rocks ablaze with light and the waves of a glowing sea, simple people and splendid people, visions of awe and splendour, gentle, charming figments and hallucinatory apparitions, prancing centaurs, fairy-goddesses in trailing gowns come and go, silent, gentle, passionate, wild—the painter's dream is haunted by the age-old dreams and nightmares and the contemplation of serene and supreme reality." This great artist, as resistant to classification as Puvis de Chavannes, though for different reasons, was not recognised by his contemporaries till comparatively late in his life, but his fame was all the greater since it came from the appreciation of Mallarmé and Huysmans. Durand-Ruel, who had discovered him in 1895, exhibited his works right until his death. He had exhibitions abroad during his lifetime, from 1908 onwards, in Amsterdam, London and New York.

Rossetti, Dante-Gabriel (1828-82)

English painter and poet born in London. His father was Italian and came to England to escape the persecutions of Ferdinand, King of the Two Sicilies. The young Rossetti studied design at the Royal Academy. A few years later he associated himself with Holman Hunt, Millais, Thomas Woolner, James Collinson and F. G. Stephens: in this way, Pre-Raphaelitism was born. Ruskin gave it his blessing. In 1852, Rossetti married the beautiful Miss Siddal who posed for many of his pictures and represented his ideal of beauty in art and in poetry. She died two years later and his grief was very great. His paintings can be seen in New York (Metropolitan Museum), London (National Gallery, Tate Gallery, National Portrait Gallery and Victoria and Albert Museum) and other European museums.

Rousseau, Théodore (1812-67)

French painter and engraver, born in Paris, died in Barbizon. He started work in the studio of his cousin, Paul de Saint-Martin, who soon realised how talented the young artist was. From this period we have *View of the Cemetery and the Telegraph Post at Montmartin*. He began to specialise in landscapes and his real fame dates from this time; he travelled about the country, painting out of doors in Compiègne, in the Chevreuse valley, on the banks of the Seine. He went to the Auvergne and Provence. He had a very original approach and was attacked by Classical painters, which brought him disfavour in the eyes of the general public and spoiled his chances for the Salon. He went to paint in the forest of Fontainebleau where he painted landscapes all through the year. But he was too fine a painter to be ignored and his work became more and more appreciated in Paris. A whole room was devoted to his work at the 1855 Exhibition.

Turner, William (1775-1851)

English painter, water-colourist and engraver, born and died in London. His father was a barber; his mother went mad a few years after he was born. William Turner was amazingly precocious as an artist—as early as the age of nine, he was drawing superbly. He studied eagerly and was admitted to the Royal Academy school when he was fourteen. Elected academician at twenty-seven (in 1802). His artistic skill and his reputation grew. He travelled in Italy, France and Germany, bringing back views of Venice which count as some of the finest ever painted. His range of skills was vast—he was a superb portrait-painter, a master of seascapes, a matchless water-colourist and an engraver of originality. It was in the treatment of landscapes that he excelled, however, particularly in the fresh and original way he painted. He gave them a dreamlike quality which makes them incomparable.